WONDER VERSE

Pages From The Playground

First published in Great Britain in 2025 by:

 YoungWriters® ——— Est. 1991 ——

Young Writers
Remus House
Coltsfoot Drive
Peterborough
PE2 9BF
Telephone: 01733 890066
Website: www.youngwriters.co.uk

FOREWORD

WELCOME READER,

For Young Writers' latest competition *Wonderverse*, we asked primary school pupils to explore their creativity and write a poem on any topic that inspired them. They rose to the challenge magnificently with some going even further and writing stories too! The result is this fantastic collection of writing in a variety of styles.

Here at Young Writers our aim is to encourage creativity in children and to inspire a love of the written word, so it's great to get such an amazing response, with some absolutely fantastic pieces. This open theme of this competition allowed them to write freely about something they are interested in, which we know helps to engage kids and get them writing. Within these pages you'll find a variety of topics, from hopes, fears and dreams, to favourite things and worlds of imagination. The result is a collection of brilliant writing that showcases the creativity and writing ability of the next generation.

I'd like to congratulate all the young writers in this anthology, I hope this inspires them to continue with their creative writing.

CONTENTS

Bhavya Kota (8) 54

Grateley Primary School, Grateley

Scarlett Way (10) 55
Felix Way (7) 56

Heaton Avenue Primary School, Cleckheaton

Veronica Campisi (10) 57
Willow Williams (9) 58
Charlotte Hogg (9) 59
Khadija Antulay (9) 60
Mollie Louise Cooper (10) 61
Lillie Cooper (10) 62
Elena Tolikas (10) 63

Landkey Community Primary Academy, Landkey

Harriet Perrin (10) 64
Leah Felicio (9) 65
Caitlin O'Donnell (9) 66
Poppy King (10) 67

Markeaton Primary School, Derby

Freya Knowles (10) 68
Caden Rae-Eldret (9) 69
Rose Lyon (10) 70
Oscar Child (10) 72
Nellie Stone (9) 74
Alessandro Gherardi (9) 75
Maxie Green (10) 76
Lennon McNulty (9) 77
Lilly Trend (9) 78
Hanna Iwasieczko (10) 79
Harry Hobday (9) 80
Lyla Martin (9) 81
Evie Read (10) 82
Lottie Brown (10) 83
Ruby-Esme Beresford (10) 84
Luca Camp (9) 85

Mia Jones (10) 86
Isaac Bearn (10) 87
Arlo Foster (9) 88
Caspar Rae-Eldret (9) 89
Lincoln Rhodes (10) 90
Zachary O'Haolain (10) 91
Gracie Barry (10) 92
Remai O'Connor (10) 93
Max Lubinski (10) 94
Albert Cole (9) 95
Sami Smyth-Omar (10) 96
Seth Clark 97
Alice Miles (9) 98
Aliyana Macfarlane (9) 99
Lucie Webb (10) 100
Elliott Kinnear (10) 101
Ariana Evans (10) 102
Arthur Stone (9) 103
William Johnstone (10) 104
Rudra Ashwin (10) 105
Arthur Toogood (10) 106
Toby Lince (10) 107
Jack Rose (10) 108
Jack Rothwell (10) 109

Mayflower Community Academy, Plymouth

Lexi Deacon (7) 110
Thea Shurmer (7) 111
Mariana Jannetta (7) 112
Daniella Babatunde (7) 113
Abi Edworthy (7) 114

Queen's Gate Junior School, London

Harmony Chen (8) 115
Lily Hurst (7) 116
Evelyn Marini-Goodwin (7) 117

Saffron Green Primary School, Borehamwood

Alexandra Stranis (8)	118
Sophia Maria Botosanu (9)	119
Alaya Neophytou (9)	120

Sheen Mount Primary School, Sheen

Poppy du Parcq (11)	121
Cinar Ozcan (11)	122
Eric Net (11)	123
Charlotte Boyd (10)	124
Florence Ferrer (10)	126
Ryan Price (11)	127
Alexandra Kaoullas (11)	128

Shipbourne School, Shipbourne

Ivy Brown (7)	129
Eleanor Walton (8)	130
Alistair Gibbon (8)	132
Zara Lyons (8)	133
Jasmine Fox (8)	134
James Ruse (8)	135
Joey Levett (8)	136

St Joseph's Catholic Primary School, Thame

Poppy Strike (9)	137
Toby Partner (9)	138
Florrie Hollis (9)	139
Theia Perry (9)	140
Maeve Talbot (9)	141
Gabriela Glazer (9)	142
Ashlee Sinclair (9)	143
Katy Wright (9)	144
Jasper Darby (9)	145
Stanley Quin (8)	146
Milan Iojica (9)	147
Benji Jurik (9)	148
James Constant (8)	149
Jack Andre Arthur Markham (9)	150

Max Weller (9)	151
Juliet Peddle (9)	152
Thomas Carpenter (9)	153
Alex Karpovych (9)	154
Matilda Stubbs (9)	155

St Nicholas CE (VA) Primary School And Nursery, Stevenage

Maddison Crook (9)	156
Sara Szilagyi (9)	158
Poppy Lasenby (9)	160
Ming Yee Tsang (8)	161
Ella Fawibe (9)	162
Pyper De Jager (9)	163
Estera Vasiliu (8)	164
Brodie Coveney (8)	165
Milo Cleverdon (9)	166
Angel Ayomide Ojo (9)	167

Ulceby St Nicholas Church Of England Primary School, Ulceby

Hollie Jenkins (11)	168
Maisie Webb (11)	169
Edward Paul (11)	170
Oscar Montgomery (11)	171
Tilly Butler (10)	172
Trystan Reed (11)	173
Oakley Whall (11)	174
Ollie Cade (10)	175
Jessica Ransom (10)	176
Oscar Greer (10)	177
Willow Zergi (10)	178
Ellie-Rose Whitham (11)	179
Jorgie Lewis (10)	180
Sebastian Drozdowicz (10)	181
Josh Easton (9)	182
Roman Cowie (10)	183
Henry Greer (9)	184
Theo Butler (10)	185
Bailey Hinchliffe (9)	186
Mason Stearman (9)	187
Sophie Spicer (9)	188

Woodham Ley Primary School, Great Tarpots

Jessica Lee (9)   189

THE CREATIVE WRITING

Type 1 Superhero

Sometimes, my diabetes makes me sad,
Sometimes, it makes me really mad,
When my blood sugar is in range,
It makes me feel extremely glad.

When I eat carbs, it shoots up high,
My glucose numbers hit the sky,
When I go low, dizzy I'll go,
I feel so awful I could cry.

Some people think it's caused by my diet,
I wish that they would just be quiet,
My body has attacked itself,
My silly pancreas caused a riot.

Despite all this, I've been so brave,
The needles, the finger pricks, I never cave.
I always stay so, so strong,
No matter what comes along.

I have a sensor I have to wear,
Some people might stop and stare,
But it helps to keep me alive and well,
So I really do not even care.

I am a Type 1 superhero!

Finlay Smith (9)
Aberdare Park Primary School, Trecynon

Echoes Of Murrayfield

In bonnie Scotland, where Murrayfield abides,
Lies the ball dolf flies, an thy echoes does aye ride.
Murrayfield's steamin' wi' cheer an' pride
Wi Gaelic roars that cannae hide.
Like lions, we shout, oor kilts held high,
Flags are flying 'gainst the sky.
The thistles wave, the pipes gan wild,
Every Scot frae man to child.
Murrayfield Stadium echoes oor wee hearts ay
thumpin, crowds ae singin' wae oor feet ay jumpin'.
Oor unlucky enemy always received a pumpin'.
Frae the pitch, tae city streets, that braw loud echo,
They aw cannae beat wae the bagpipes gan,
Clap yer hauns 'n' stomp yer toes,
'Cos Scottish thunder never rains on oor parade,
A wa' as big Hadrian a forward drive,
The crowd holds its breath, oh we're aw feelin' alive,
Tackles so sharp, tries soe braw, wee laddies cheer,
and we've won the war.

In bonnie Scotland,
Where Murrayfield lies, the ball dolf flies,
And echoes arise.
Murrayfield filled with cheers and pride,
Gaelic roars as loud as loud lions with
Kilts and flags, proudest we've ever been.
The thistle waves while the bagpipes are blasting,
The Scottish fans are lasting.
Scottish pride on display, home or away.
Clap your hands, stomp your feet,
Murrayfield echoes will greet.
From the stadium, to the streets.
A solid wall, a forward drive comes,
The stadium is numb,
Here comes the final scrum.
Tackles so fierce, tries are grand,
Hold on wee boys, we've won for our land.

Jake Riddiford (8)
Aberdare Park Primary School, Trecynon

Content:

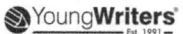

The Travelling Mouse

This is the story of a travelling mouse.
He travelled through time
To a Tudor merchant's house.
The house was wood, and the roof was straw,
What an amazing sight he saw!
There was a family of eight
Who inside, slept, worked and ate.
From Henry VIII to Elizabeth I,
They could have been worse.
It was great to see what they lived like,
As long as their heads didn't end up on a spike!

Elizabeth Davenport (8)
Aberdare Park Primary School, Trecynon

4

I Am A Beautiful Unicorn

I have a magical horn
I've had it since I was born

I sparkle and shine in the sun
I fly so high and have lots of fun
With my friends, I like to run

I'm always happy and never sad
When you see me, you'll be glad
I'll be the best friend you've ever had

I like to eat popsicles
And riding my special bicycle
And the island where I live is tropical.

Seren Cottle (9)
Aberdare Park Primary School, Trecynon

Animals Around The World

Lions
The lion's mane is like a fluffy crown
As loud as a vacuum cleaner
Roar!

Meerkat
A meerkat is as skinny
As a stick man
Like a golden sun swooshing
Around the world.
Swoosh.

Monkey
The monkey is like
A gymnast swinging through the
Air
As brown as chocolate
That I eat at the fair
Chomp.

Scarlett Harris (9)
Aberdare Park Primary School, Trecynon

School Day

Early start, rise and shine
Yet another learning time
We go to school to be our best
When all we want to do is rest
I love school and all it brings
Because I enjoy learning new things
Smiling from ear to ear
While making our way through year to year
Playtime is our favourite time, when us, as friends, have fun
But it won't be long before another school day is done.

Iwan Parker Thomas (8)
Aberdare Park Primary School, Trecynon

Summer Is The Best Season

Summertime is so much fun,
Everyone smiles when they see the sun.

Sandy toes, smiley faces, and lots of visits to seaside places.
Building sandcastles, finding seashells, and watching sunsets make me happy.

There is so much to do, even enjoying a family BBQ.
Summertime is the best, as in most places, it gives the rain clouds a rest.

Summer is the best season!

Elsie-Rose Thomas (9)
Aberdare Park Primary School, Trecynon

The Amazon Rainforest

The leaves are as green as vomit,
The sky is as blue as sapphire eyes,
The river is as beautiful as this school.

The layers are as dangerous as a lion, hungry!
The people are as scared as a mouse being chased.
The animals are as hungry as a homeless person.

Harper Prichard (9)
Aberdare Park Primary School, Trecynon

Green Ribbon

M indful
E motions
N otice
T alk
A wareness
L isten

H elp
E xercise
A nxiety
L earn
T herapy
H ope

It's okay not to be okay.

Jacob Ellis (9)
Aberdare Park Primary School, Trecynon

Nature

N ature in the sapphire-blue sky
A nimals are chirping and singing
T errific, wonderful, emerald forests
U nstoppable, fantastic trees
R uby, gleaming roses
E legant, flying birds.

Elena Chernykh (8)
Aberdare Park Primary School, Trecynon

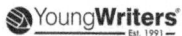
Cousin Friendship

Friendships are the best
And I have lots and lots,
Mine and my cousin's is special,
We're best together, like a pair of socks,
We play, we share, we do each other's hair
Style each other with bows and knots,
Then, after, we play Roblox,
Friendships are the best,
I love my cousins lots and lots like Jelly Tots.

Kizmay Payne-Uranie (8)
Abington Vale Primary School, Cliftonville

Family

F amily is fun to spend time with
A nd there are lots of games to choose from
M ums, dads and brothers are playful
I n the house you live in
L oving and caring is what you should be
Y earning to help your parents, after you finish
    playing!

Haneef Swallah (9)

Abington Vale Primary School, Cliftonville

The Sun

The sun is good,
The sun is round,
Oh, sun, give us light.
The sun is a big fireball,
The sun provides light.
Oh, sun, shine on me
This very day!
The sun glows
In the clear blue sky,
The sun is hot,
Oh, sun, give energy,
For we need it!

Aseda Agyenim Boateng (9)
Abington Vale Primary School, Cliftonville

The Dark

The dark shines in its own way,
Even though it is grey.
Its beauty cannot be explained,
It's like a show with no escape.
The dark hums a quiet tune,
A velvet cloak beneath the moon.
It holds secrets lost in time,
And echoes like a lullaby's rhyme.

Christina Sowonoye (9)
Abington Vale Primary School, Cliftonville

Animals And Nature

A nimals hunting species
N ature killing, nature living
I llegal to kill, please save animals
M ost land, some other
A nimals living, someday die
L egal to save, please do
S ome regular, one special.

Matvii Fesak (9)
Abington Vale Primary School, Cliftonville

Summer's Embrace

On a beautiful summer day,
Where a wonderful girl lays
Beneath the bright sun's golden rays,
She dreams and laughs in a carefree haze.
By the sparkling shore where the cool waves play,
She dances and spins in her joyful ballet.
Under the azure sky, in a lush green bay,
She whispers secrets, the gentle breezes sway.
In the warm fragrant breeze, as the children all play,
She basks in the glow of the sun's golden ray.
With ice cream in hand and her friends all in sway,
She smiles in the light of a perfect summer day.
Under the clear blue sky, where the sea birds survey,
She laughs and she twirls in her carefree ballet.
With the scent of the flowers and the ocean's spray,
She treasures each moment of her joyful summer day.

Bella Walker (10)
Beechcroft St Paul's CE (VA) Primary School, Weymouth

Roots And Wings

In the garden of life,
Where wild wings
Flow through the sky,
Friendship and family
Light the way.
Roots that run deep
In the soft, rich Earth.
Wings that give dreams,
And laughter,
Birth, family,
The place where the heart first learns
Through seasons of change,
Through love that burns.
Their voices are echoes
Of all we have known.
Their hands are clasped
When we are alone,
And friendship,
Sweet friendship,
Butterflies gleam.
A bridge in the darkness,
A thread through a dream.

Chosen peers,
Who dance through the years,
Sharing our greatest achievement,
Softening fears.
Together,
They create us a shelter,
A song,
A place where
We know we belong.
Through storms,
And through sunlight,
And through starlight,
Family and friendship,
Our treasure most dear.

Lexi Heelis (11)
Beechcroft St Paul's CE (VA) Primary School, Weymouth

Emotions

Happy and calm,
Smiling at my alarm!
Stopped thinking, *Oh darn*,
Laughed so hard, I felt like a ringing alarm!
Some other days...
Tears streaming down my face with anger and rage!
Mostly anxious and stressed,
But also embarrassed,
And energetic, how happy is the little stone...
That rambles down the road alone,
And doesn't care about careers,
And never fears,
Whose coat of elemental brown,
A passing universe put on,
And as independent as the sun,
Associates or glows alone?

Ellie-Mai Brown (10)
Beechcroft St Paul's CE (VA) Primary School, Weymouth

The Seasons

Winter, spring, summer, fall,
There are seasons, four in all.
Here we go, around the year again,
To greet the different seasons.
Winter is time for snow,
To the south, the birds will go.
Spring, a time when flowers bloom,
And birds groom.
Summertime, the days are hot,
Too much to rot.
It's fall now, it's now cool,
I guess time for school.
Around the year, one more time.

Olivia Hutchinson (11)
Beechcroft St Paul's CE (VA) Primary School, Weymouth

Painting

Let paint take you for a ride,
Tunnel of art inside
A magical world of a pen,
Pencil, paintbrush, wooden men,
Pencil on paper,
Watercolours equal water vapour.

As the colours dry,
A pretty painting,
Me oh my,
This art that I have made
Is priceless, not to trade.

A world full of art to draw
Is many dreams galore!

Dayna Sharrock (11)
Claygate Primary School, Claygate

Look Through The Window

The wind twists and turns in your hair,
The sea is splashing everywhere,
And that's when you realise life's not fair,
For the wind is harsh, but the sun's still shining,
Making a path that's twisted and winding,
Every day, a new cog turns,
Either stunning and blinding or silently hiding,
Turning, clashing, bashing and scratching,
Until each one is finally matching.

Life is at its end. Life is a new beginning,
Life is a very long journey that we are now living.

Imogen Pegler (10)
Crudwell CE Primary School, Malmesbury

Find Your Feeling

I smile and clap my hands,
Jumping around like a bunny.
My heart fills with laughter,
I'm so happy.
What emotion am I?

Answer: Joy.

I sing out loud
And I get praised.
I fill up with smiles,
What emotion am I?

Answer: Happiness.

Some words may upset me,
I flood with tears down my face.
My body starts to shake,
And my bottom lip starts to quiver.
What emotion am I?

Answer: Sadness.

I light up when I get presents,
I jump up and down.
I can't even calm myself down,
And I can't stop smiling.
What emotion am I?

Answer: Excitement.

Hattie David (11)
Crudwell CE Primary School, Malmesbury

Awesome Animals

In the jungle,
I can see
A roaring tiger,
Hungry for tea!

Also climbing
In the tree,
Is a monkey,
Big as can be!

In the meadow,
I can spy
A cute bunny
Hopping by!

Buzzing in the
Sunset sky,
Is a rainbow
Butterfly!

In the forest,
Over there,
Is a great big
Grizzly bear!

Suddenly,
A fox runs by
Trying to chase
An ugly black fly!

In the field,
Running near,
Is a jolly
Baby deer!

Also in the field
Right now,
Is a giant
Highland cow!

Esmae Jones (11)
Crudwell CE Primary School, Malmesbury

She Is Space

I am darker than the night sky
Though I am prettier than anyone I know
My white freckles decorate the midnight sky
As my friends surround me always

I am dark but my friends light the way
My sister is always beside me, helping me
Most of my friends are old, some are young
One's boiling hot and one colder than anything

There is more of me out there
But you may never know
The question is
How far will you go?

Elodie Lowe (10)
Crudwell CE Primary School, Malmesbury

The Owl

The owl's eyes twinkled
As it swooped down low,
The forest air mingled
With freshly fallen snow.

Its feathers were deep brown
As the moonlight caught them,
Wings didn't make a sound
As it began falling.

It pounced on its prey,
And that was that,
The end of the day
For the owl acrobat.

Lana Cooper (10)
Crudwell CE Primary School, Malmesbury

Black Cat

I see a black cat cross my path
Its fur shines like silk
In the sun's warm glow.
I see it as neither good nor bad
But just a cat that crossed my path.

Ada Breen (10)

Crudwell CE Primary School, Malmesbury

Dogs

Dogs.
Playful, naughty and full of energy!
Hiding toys, toileting everywhere, causing chaos all the time!
The best pet ever, but also... the worst!
Have you seen them bite?
Have you heard them bark?
Have you seen them snarl?
Dogs.
Playful, loving and full of energy!
Always happy, shedding everywhere, cuddles forever and ever.
The best pet you could ever have, but take your chances.
Have you seen them cuddle?
Have you heard them sing?
Have you seen them lick?
Dogs.
A friend you can trust and always rely on,
And someone you know you can lean on in sad or worrying times,
And even times you just need a cuddle.
A companion forever and will protect you and be there for you always.

Rose Bacon (9)
Eye CE Primary School, Eye

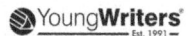

The Wonders Of Space

Is space an ethereal place where stars dance around?
Is space an endless sea of stars going past black holes?
Is space an empty place where stars are far away?
These are the wonders of space.
Is space an endless place where planets orbit the sun?
Is space a vacuum where it's perfect and silent?
Is space somewhere to call home?
These are the wonders of space.

Alessia-Ioana Popa (9)
Eye CE Primary School, Eye

Death Has Arrived

Friendship doesn't last forever
Certainly not here
Instead, there is death
The sound of scraping knives haunts the houses
The graveyard is full of dead
The ghosts play, screaming in the dead of night
They run freely
A murderer runs with them
The blood-dripping knives drop to the ground
A light beams down
A new ghost has arrived.

Mia Kennard (10)
Eye CE Primary School, Eye

Invisible Adrian

Adrian had a secret
He didn't want to share.
One day, he was just a boy
Who liked to play with a toy.

Adrian had a wish
While he was eating a dish.
He wanted to be invisible
So no one could see him.
While Adrian blew out his birthday candle,
He shouted as loud as a lion,
"I want to be invisible as a ghost!"

The next day,
When he woke up,
He looked in the mirror,
And he couldn't see himself.
He did see
His wish had come true.

Down the stairs he ran,
To scare his mum,
And then he said, "Mum, rah!"
And scared his mum,
And Adrian laughed
As hard as a motorbike.

But a splash of water
Landed on Adrian,
And at that moment,
He became visible.

From that moment,
Adrian knew
That if he wanted to be invisible,
All he had to do was to say,
"I want to be invisible."

Adrian Sabo (8)
Faraday School, Poplar

All About The Special Seasons!

All of the seasons are unique,
Winter is the word that goes from tree to tree,
Spring is sweet like strawberries,
Summer is super like sugar and
Autumn is amazing, like getting an award!

In the seasons, we all have special hobbies,
Like building a large, maybe very large, snowman in winter,
Planting seeds in some dirt in the spring,
Going to the beach in sunny summer,
And crushing leaves in autumn.

I love winter as it is Christmas and New Year,
I enjoy seeing the flowers blossom in spring because it is beautiful,
I love summer since it is sunny and the end of school,
I enjoy autumn as it is my birthday and, of course, the spooky season.

In the seasons, there are months, for example,
December, January and February are in winter,
March, April and May are in spring,
June, July and August are in summer,
September, October and November are in autumn!

Alexis Jones (8)
Faraday School, Poplar

Waiting

There's a cave on the hill where the cold winds race.
And something lives there - you won't see its face.
It growls in the dark and watches at night,
But it hides from the sun and avoids the light.
No one has seen it, for it stays in its lair,
Yet footprints appear when there's mist in the air.
Its eyes, they say, are shimmering green,
And it watches the world, though it's never been seen.
It never comes out, not even to play,
It just hums to itself and sleeps through the day.
Some say it's lonely, some say it's wise,
But all we can see is the glint of its eyes.
So if you walk near, tread soft and beware,
The creature is waiting, but won't leave its lair.
It listens, it watches, it gleams and it waits,
Behind the dark mouth of the old iron gate.

Deia Lam-Fairburn (10)
Faraday School, Poplar

Mine And Eva's Friendship

M e and Eva in our garden
I have Roblox and Eva does as well
A nd we play together

A lso, we play Brookhaven
N ext, we play talent shows
D on't run away, Eva

E va has a little Squishmallow
V ery cold, we huddle together
A nd then it gets... warm
S o, let's get inside before it gets cold

F un with Eva
R un around in the house, play Tag
I n five minutes
E va has to go
N ext, she has to go in thirty seconds
"D on't go," I say
S he has ten seconds to go
H er mum calls and says she is an hour away
I jump with joy
P ut out, then her mum comes.

Mia-Rae Fenton-Boriel (8)
Faraday School, Poplar

The Seasons

In spring, the flowers start to bloom,
The sun shines bright, it chases gloom.
Birds sing sweetly in the trees,
And gentle winds dance with the breeze.

Summer comes with sunny days,
We splash in pools and laugh and play.
Ice cream melts upon my tongue,
The days are long and songs are sung.

Then autumn paints the leaves in gold,
With crunchy paths and stories told.
The pumpkins grow, the harvest's here,
We jump in piles with lots of cheers!

When winter comes, the world is white,
With snowflakes twirling in the light.
We build a snowman, oh so tall,
And cosy up with fun for all!

Sophia Brewster (8)
Faraday School, Poplar

The Hummingbird Went To The Store

The hummingbird went to the store,
But was sad because he was poor,
He sat on the chair,
For he felt despair,
He couldn't buy cheese anymore!

The pizza he'd prepped was not done,
And eating it would be no fun,
For this sad old bird,
It would be absurd
To serve up this meal to his chum.

The bird's friend was a piglet called Wyatt,
Who had been sat there ever so quiet,
But to the feathery chef,
He oinked so loud you'd go deaf,
"No thanks! I'm on a diet!"

Ada Ellis-Jones (8)
Faraday School, Poplar

Dear Mum, From The Mud

Dear Mum, I miss your meat and mash,
I miss the dog, I miss my splash.
The boots are big, the bed is cold,
But I stay brave, I must be bold.

The bombs go *bang!* The guns go *boom!*
The skies are dark, not much of a moon.
We march in mud, we march all day.
I think of home to chase away.

I write with hope, I write with heart,
From far away, but not apart.
I fight for peace, for skies of blue,
Dear Mum, I fight for me and you.

Yaseen Saeed (8)
Faraday School, Poplar

My Big, Enormous Dream

When I grow up, I want to be a pro player at West Ham United. West Ham is my dream to play with when I'm older because I have signed a professional contract for them. When I grow up, I will be the best player for West Ham since I have lots of training sessions. I might be very good, but I don't know. As I will be a pro, I can get lots of money, so I need to work hard every single day. Next, I will not stop football in my whole, entire life. This big, enormous dream. A professional.

Malik Bolenga (7)
Faraday School, Poplar

When The Next Pirates Come

When the next pirates come,
Gone will be the rum,
In their tummies
And next to be mummies.

When these pirates come,
They will invade,
They will neither give,
Nor will they trade.

They are filled with greed,
They will take the things you need.

The pirates search high and low,
When they find it,
They'll take the treasure and go.

Zahra Chowdhury (9)
Faraday School, Poplar

Space Station

We went up far, far away and reached space,
We went so fast, like we were in a race,
We reached the station, which we would call home,
We wanted to call Mum and Dad, but there was no phone,
We couldn't get back because the rocket was broken,
But have no fear because I'm Aramis Pokun!
We stayed in space for a year and a day,
We finally got back in the month of May.

Aramis Pokun (9)
Faraday School, Poplar

Faraday

F araday is my school
A nd when I was young, I wasn't very tall
R ound the corner was a big, red boat
A pples and pears lying in the yard
D ogs are lying in the yard, looking at the Shard
A way from the school is a little coffee shop
Y ou won't believe Andy makes coffee with a mop!

Sonny Ciacharowski (8)
Faraday School, Poplar

Bear

Little face, tiny nose.
Super playful, then having a doze.
Soft as silk, sweet as pie.
Biting on everything but not knowing why.
He's got four mini paws and a big soft heart.
I hate every second that we are apart.
My best friend, my buddy, we're always together.
My puppy and me, I'll love you forever.

Titus Boniface (8)
Faraday School, Poplar

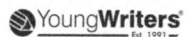

Me And My BFF Mia

Me and Mia, running around the park.
Me and Mia, together, unstoppable.
Me and Mia, constantly chatting every day.
Me and Mia, always playing with each other.
Me and Mia, I always have a few dreams about Mia.
Me and Mia are unstoppable and I love her,
She is my best friend, forever and ever.

Eva Hanif (8)
Faraday School, Poplar

Monkeys

M onkeys swing from tree to tree,
O n branches wild and free.
N ibbling fruit and having fun,
K icking leaves and on the run!
E very day's a jungle game,
Y ou can't catch them, they're never tame.
S illy, speedy, smart - that's them!

Eva Irina Despa (7)
Faraday School, Poplar

The Seaside

At the sea,
Big waves crash,
People swim,
Jump and laugh.

Turquoise waves,
Glowing plankton,
Purple sunset,
Distant waves.

The sea,
The sea,
A wonderful place
To swim and dive,
Build up your pace.

The sea.

Meera Inkinen (8)
Faraday School, Poplar

Space Adventure

S taring at the infinite night sky,
P lanets circling up high,
A deep desire sparkled in me to fly,
C limbing up in the rocket, filled with fear and joy,
E ntering space for a new adventure.

Neel Swetha Prakash (7)

Faraday School, Poplar

Friend

F riends are special.

w **R** ecks can happen.

I gnoring and leaving out. But

w **E** can change it around.

N ever leave out. You

D eserve friends.

Eva Haggarly (8)
Faraday School, Poplar

Summer

I like summer, summer
You like the sun, sun
I like the bloom, bloom
You like the moon, moon
Summer is so much fun, fun
Fun is happy in the sun, sun.

Wolf Thorne (8)
Faraday School, Poplar

Lion

L ion fur is as soft as a pillow,
I n the grass, hides an armadillo,
O n a tree, a monkey sits,
N oticing a butterfly that flits.

Bhavya Kota (8)
Faraday School, Poplar

A Greek Tragedy

Lightning strikes, thunder roars,
Waves crash and death pours,
Misery lurks and joy dissolves,
Thanatos smirks in a sea of skulls,

Happiness burns and despair replaces,
Who is the answer to these lethal cases?
Achilles rises from the fields of Elysium,
The Greeks' most prominent hero,

Eyes of gold, muscles of rock,
Lays waste to his foes,
Masks his fright, no fear he shows,
World War III seems to have started,
Greek and Roman ways have parted.

Scarlett Way (10)
Grateley Primary School, Grateley

Pokémon Fight!

P ika punch (attack from Pikachu EX.)

O bliviates his opponents

K ick, punch, defend, Pikachu knocks out his opponent

"E ee!" shouts Pikachu's opponent. Pikachu is too scary

M ega Charizard X stomps in, roaring, but Pikachu isn't scared.

"O bliviate Pikachu," says Charizard's trainer

"N o," says Pikachu, and knocks out Mega Charizard X.

Felix Way (7)
Grateley Primary School, Grateley

Best Friends!

It was my first day of nursery. I didn't know anyone there until I saw a little girl sitting on a bench alone. I was too shy to go up to her, but then I thought to myself, *I can do this! I am brave.*

So then I went up to her and said happily, "Hey, you seem lonely, do you want to be friends?" She stopped for a second to think. I was a bit confused at first because I thought she was going to answer straight away.

But right after I thought that, she screamed as loud as she could, *"Yes!"* I asked her what her name was and she said, "Sophia, what's yours?"

"Amy."

Now we were in Year 1. Me and Sophia were so happy that we were growing so fast. The next day, me and Sophia had a playdate and we did so much together.

Veronica Campisi (10)
Heaton Avenue Primary School, Cleckheaton

The Way Of Life

You start off with no care whatsoever,
But soon, you become more clever.
Going to nursery,
Happily,
That's the way of life.
On your way to primary school,
To then in Year 6, think you're too cool.
Now you're so intelligent,
You think you're a secret agent,
That's the way of life.
You've had eight six-week holidays,
Now only five left to go.
In high school,
Some of your friends may have gone to a different
school,
But you can make new ones,
And bake buns in food economics class,
That's the way of life.
You have graduated from uni, but there is still much
more ahead.

Willow Williams (9)
Heaton Avenue Primary School, Cleckheaton

Space Wanders

In a quiet embrace of the universe,
Aliens whisper secrets
Through the endless black hole.

Galaxies twist and turn like dancers,
Spinning until they die.
Every alien has a blend of dreams,
Like a picture they painted by time.

Planets spin around the sun,
But on Uranus and Neptune, they rain diamonds.
All of the aliens gather round to catch a diamond or two.

But in that crazy atmosphere,
We are just whispers on Earth.

So we gaze at the moon at night,
That gives so much delight.
Just remember, we are never alone,
There are other planets too.

Charlotte Hogg (9)
Heaton Avenue Primary School, Cleckheaton

Space

I am high
In the sky
If you want to get to me
You'll have to fly
What am I?

T he solar system
H ome to all the planets
E arth is where we live

Up, up, up in the sky
There are eight planets
There used to be nine planets
But Pluto is too small
It is a dwarf planet
And not in our solar system

S olar system
P lanets
A nd stars
C an be seen from space
E ven though it may be tricky.

Khadija Antulay (9)
Heaton Avenue Primary School, Cleckheaton

Emotion Tree

Emotion is what we feel,
It's deep down inside.
It sprouts like a tree within you and I.
I'm happy when I'm smiling,
I'm sad when I'm crying,
But everyone does.
Everyone has emotions,
It's how we express all of our feelings,
Happy, sad, angry, jealous, anxiety and
embarrassment.
We all feel emotions a lot.
Emotion trees grow in all of us and show the best.

Mollie Louise Cooper (10)
Heaton Avenue Primary School, Cleckheaton

Friends Are Friends, Family Is Forever!

Friends are for along the way,
Family is forever.
Family will stay by you forever,
Through rain and snow.
Friends will hurt you when they get the chance,
You will understand when you grow up.
Family will stay by you through rain and snow,
Even when it hurts!
Time and time again, sorrow and hate can take over,
And take your love for the people you show affection
to.

Lillie Cooper (10)
Heaton Avenue Primary School, Cleckheaton

Space

Galaxies twisting and turning like fish in the oceans,
The colours are like potions,
Rockets are roaring,
As the spaceship is soaring,
Neptune is small like the moon,
The black hole is full of doom,
Space is big and dark,
Stars are yellow like sparks.

Elena Tolikas (10)
Heaton Avenue Primary School, Cleckheaton

Dog Nap

There in the corner lies a little black dog,
She is soft and fluffy and plays all day.
When she gets food, she yells, "Hip, hip, hooray!"
She's had a hard day playing with her friends,
She slowly closes her eyes as her day nicely ends.
She wakes up in the morning, feeling very sprightly,
And she goes out in the garden where the sun shines brightly.
She plays and she plays until she starts to yawn,
So she goes back to bed and closes her eyes tightly.

Harriet Perrin (10)
Landkey Community Primary Academy, Landkey

Autumn

The leaves are falling as
Summer fades. The ground
Is painted in multiple shades.

The birds have packed and already
Gone. Somewhere distant, somewhere
Warm.

My woolly hat is out, and so is my
Fleece, to keep me warm from the
Northern breeze.

I can't go out to play, it's a
Miserable day. So I will lie in
My bed and write a poem instead!

Leah Felicio (9)
Landkey Community Primary Academy, Landkey

Everest

At a death-defying height
All turn back in fright

Snow whizzes past me
My breathing shallow

The oxygen running low
As I get blinded by the snow

My legs shaking
My body aching

Dragging my feet
I accept defeat.

Caitlin O'Donnell (9)
Landkey Community Primary Academy, Landkey

Winter

Crunching snow beneath your feet,
Water frozen, over a metre deep,
Snow piled high, very steep,
The presents under the tree are yours to keep,
The season's almost over, but no need to weep,
The sun is coming out, and so are the sheep!

Poppy King (10)
Landkey Community Primary Academy, Landkey

Unique

When I look to the stars, I see that they're all different,
Each one of them unique, like us,
In a crowd, we all stand out.

Only when we shine, we stand out,
Our courage blazes in our hearts,
In a crowd, we all stand out.

We should appreciate other people's differences,
Everybody should be proud of who they are,
In a crowd, we all stand out.

Our identities should be celebrated,
Because the world grows brighter when our differences
are honoured,
In a crowd, we all stand out.

Each one of us plays a different part in our world,
When we turn the page, we turn to another person,
In a crowd, we all stand out.

Freya Knowles (10)
Markeaton Primary School, Derby

Everyone But Me

Everyone here is an amazing gamer,
Everyone here is amazing at football,
Everyone here has a house full of technology,
Everyone here has parents who can afford nice clubs,
Everyone here has loads of money,
Everyone here has a life with sweets guaranteed,
Everyone here has a feast for every meal,
Everyone here has brothers and sisters who aren't mean,
Everyone here has loads of friends,
Everyone here has parents who support them,
Everyone here has a neat and clean uniform,
Everyone here is clever and smart,
Everyone here has wonderful trips,
Everyone here has a dad...
Everyone but me.

Caden Rae-Eldret (9)
Markeaton Primary School, Derby

Time

Time slips away
As the clock chimes midnight

One day, you're running along the bay
Then you grow up
The first smile slipping away

Then you're at school
Learning football
Then you could say
I want to grow up
In some way

Next, you're at college
Learning all that knowledge

Before you know it, you've moved out
And some day, you just might say

I want to go back to that very same day

Where the trees stood still
I felt peace in the wild wood
I felt happy and good

But regretting every step
I walked away
Even though I wanted to stay.

Rose Lyon (10)
Markeaton Primary School, Derby

Bob The Champion

Bob the Bear doesn't know
What to wear
For training (Kung Fu fighting)
Getting beat
Every week
Bruised and sad
He knows he is bad
Dad's not happy
Bob the Bear knows
He needs to turn brand new
Training twice a week
Still getting beat
But getting better
Every week
Bob the Bear
About to do his first tournament after two years of
training
First match won
And when it was done
He was finally

Having fun
It came to the final
Bob the Bear
Won the war
And was declared
The champion
And got the gold
Medal.

Oscar Child (10)
Markeaton Primary School, Derby

It's Okay To Be Different

Everyone here is different to me,
I know I am unique,
I won't let them stop me,
I won't let them be mean,
I am different,
I don't care about what people think.

Everyone here has a very good life,
A life without sadness or sorrow,
But I don't care,
I am different,
I don't care about what I wear.

My skin tone,
Or hair colour,
I don't care about how I look,
As long as I feel like me.

I am me and I am unique,
I don't care about what people think,
I am me, and I am unique.

Nellie Stone (9)
Markeaton Primary School, Derby

The Spectrum Of Pride

Even shadows know their shape,
Yet the shape was not made to fit but to stand,
In the quiet, something rare begins to glow,
A flame that does not flicker in the wind.

The mountain does not ask permission to be tall,
Because the natural wonder can carry the weight of
wet snow,
One thread in fabric, unlike any other,
Need no crown; just walk broad.

A voice rises as the sun returns,
Distinct, special, different, the community has it all,
The confidence emerges - one of a kind,
It's okay to be far; you are always defined.

Alessandro Gherardi (9)
Markeaton Primary School, Derby

I Am Unique

I am unique,
I may not fit,
But I don't care,
Do this, do that,
That's air to me,
All the haters
Just need to shut up,
'Cause I don't fit,
I don't care,
If you want me to change,
Then go away,
I'm a bear
That doesn't hunt,
Am I a loser?
Am I an idiot?
No! I'm just different,
My puzzle piece doesn't fit,
Here's an idea,
Go away,
I am not afraid of what you say,
'Cause I am unique,
I am myself,
You can't change me anyway!

Maxie Green (10)
Markeaton Primary School, Derby

Mum And Son

Being kind and
Giving lots of love
Being funny and
Exchanging giggles
That's what keeps me going.

When I'm alone
She's always there
Encouraging me
When times are rough
That's what keeps me going.

She makes my breakfast
She makes my tea
Having movie nights
And staying up with me
That's what keeps me going.

Never dark
She's always light
Always courageous
She's brave and fearless
That's what keeps me going, she's my mum.

Lennon McNulty (9)
Markeaton Primary School, Derby

Growing Up

Open your eyes, little one,
I am here to guide you.
I would hold your hand every minute of every day.
But I won't because I know you have to go your own
way.
You are only four, which means you have a strong core.
But I listen and have you in my heart!
You are small but strong, young but smart.

Four years later!
Now you are eight, you can take responsibility,
And that is the best thing you can ever be.
Growing up is a hard part of life,
Now you can be the girl you have wanted to be.

Lilly Trend (9)
Markeaton Primary School, Derby

True Beauty

She thought the world would love her more
If only she could be what they adore
Prays for attention, day and night
Fading in the search of light
Hurrying with her hair and face
Then being in huge disgrace
Looking in the mirror, wanting it to erase

She goes to the mirror
To see herself clearer
But she hasn't understood
That all of her good
Is in those two eyes
Which unlocks her soul
And opens up the doorway to the heart.

That's true beauty.

Hanna Iwasieczko (10)
Markeaton Primary School, Derby

The Seasons

Summer days are here at last,
Days of school are in the past,
Ice lollies to paddling pools.
Holidays might turn grey,
Summer's warmth will fade away.
Autumn will come around,
With all the leaves on the ground.
Winter will come faster than sound,
With white or yellow snow.
Santa Claus will come to town,
With presents in your stocking.
Santa's season will come to an end,
With spring coming around,
Flowers will come and shine,
With bees buzzing around.

Harry Hobday (9)
Markeaton Primary School, Derby

Me And You Belong

When
I touch the
Snow, when I touch
The leaves, I feel so free,
I know I belong. You
Are you, and I am
Me.

Everyone
Belongs to their
Destiny. I don't care
What people say, you see
We are different in
Our own
Ways.

I can tell *you belong*,
Also, off a mountain I'll yell...
I belong!
But it's not just me, it's you...
You and you...
Who belong!

Lyla Martin (9)
Markeaton Primary School, Derby

Us

The sun is up.
The sky is blue.
I wonder how it works.
I wish magic was real.
Our true selves would be revealed.
Roses are red and violets are blue,
A gentle reminder to always be you.

When times are tough,
Through rain or shine,
The music inside you
Has a magical bind.
I wonder how we work.
Sparkles inside of you.
I bet you don't see it,
But trust me, it's true.
So suck it up and be it.

Evie Read (10)
Markeaton Primary School, Derby

The Lionesses In Space

An ordinary day at St George's Park,
Sweaty, exhausted, The Lionesses train,
The game is soon,
No luck there,
Bang, they're in the air,
In space,
Planets drop,
Bronze is there, but hits the top,
The clock is ticking,
There's no time to stop,
Now two more planets drop,
Russo strikes one,
It's...
In,
Gooaall!!
That's it,
It's finished.

Lottie Brown (10)
Markeaton Primary School, Derby

Me!

Long hair, bright and sparkling blue eyes,
Can you tell me who I'm describing?
She likes maths and also pink,
Is this who she's supposed to be?
She likes beaches, sunsets and self-care,
Also, purple, blue and yellow,
Can you guess who this is?
She likes eggs, chicken and bacon,
She's kind, helpful, smart and brave,
Inside and out!
Let me tell you who this is,
It is me!

Ruby-Esme Beresford (10)
Markeaton Primary School, Derby

Friends

Friends are kind
Friends stand with you
Through the tough times
So no matter how far you go
I hope you will know
Your friends will be with you from the start
Just put your hand on your chest
And you will feel them in your heart
Family is family
But family are also your friends
People who love you
From your head to your toes
And that will show you are perfect
No matter how you grow.

Luca Camp (9)
Markeaton Primary School, Derby

Sunny Skies

When the sun comes out,
And the sky is blue,
I'm finally outside,
Watching the tide of the sea,
Wild and free,
This is the best time for me!
I finally have some fresh air,
Doing all this without a care!

How I wish summer would last,
Those days are such a blast!
But now it's coming to an end,
How I wish it were warm,
Because now it's beginning to snow!

Mia Jones (10)
Markeaton Primary School, Derby

The Wonderverse

There is a place behind a door
In the thick of a forest
Beneath an oak, so wide and tall
Through the door into a portal
This world is strange through time and space
Grey world made of rubbish
This is our future
But there is an alternative
You're in a room
Now run out into the world
We are friendly and free
This place is amazing
This place is your heart.

Isaac Bearn (10)
Markeaton Primary School, Derby

This Is Me!

Some people like oranges,
Some people like pears,
Some people like apples,
But not me!

Some people like tennis,
Some people like football,
Some people like hockey,
But not me!

Some people like pink,
Some people like blue,
Some people like green,
But not me!

I like cherries,
I like cricket,
I like purple,
And that is me!

Arlo Foster (9)
Markeaton Primary School, Derby

Dreams

Dreams can take you anywhere,
Soaring through the sky,
From the Earth, through the skies,
Up beyond the stars,
To anywhere you want to go.
These dreams are more than memory,
These dreams are what make you, you.
Dreams take you deeper into your heart,
A wonderful place full of joy and glee,
Dreams can take you anywhere,
Dreams make you free!

Caspar Rae-Eldret (9)
Markeaton Primary School, Derby

Everyone Here Is Unique

Everyone here is unique
Liking different sports
Different brands
Or even different songs.
But the main thing is
All people are different
Some are siblings
And some are twins
Some have red hair
And others have brown hair.
But you shouldn't care
What people think of you
Because you are you
And don't let that stop you.

Lincoln Rhodes (10)
Markeaton Primary School, Derby

Identity

What makes me, me
Is on my mind,
But am I unique?
One of a kind?
All of these questions,
Thoughts are haunting my mind,
Am I funny?
Am I kind?
Identity is quite distinct,
My puzzle pieces just
Don't have links,
Should I just give up trying to find
A place where I am proud to say
I am me, and I like it that way.

Zachary O'Haolain (10)
Markeaton Primary School, Derby

Fearless

F riends forever, someone I can trust

E veryone needs someone to talk to

A chievements are my friends, so don't disrespect me

R eflect on your actions, be kind every day

L ove is not priceless

E arly life is being me

S trong and smart, unafraid

S elf-care, look after yourself and be kind!

Gracie Barry (10)

Markeaton Primary School, Derby

Kindness Doesn't Cost Anything

What makes me
Is quite distinct.
My name can
Carry the weight
Of the stars.
Pride wears no
Crown, but walks tall.
To be different is
To echo in a silent room.
Even silence has a sound
If you listen long enough.
Being kind doesn't cost anything
So pick people back up when they fall
And remember to be kind.

Remai O'Connor (10)
Markeaton Primary School, Derby

Fearless

F riends forever.

E veryone is fighting in this world.

A bove this world, there are still brave people.

R eal people are courageous.

L earn from your mistakes because people will use them.

E ach the love of a person.

S upport people, they will support you back.

S tart helping people today.

Max Lubinski (10)
Markeaton Primary School, Derby

I Am Me

A name can shine
Bright in the stars
Not to fit
D
But to stand out
My name is my name
What I think is sometimes
What I say and contribute
N
I think what I think
What I do makes me, me
A
And nothing can stop me
From being me

I am me.

Albert Cole (9)
Markeaton Primary School, Derby

My Identity

There's something different about me,
Something I think about before my tea.

Am I brave or one of a kind?
It's annoying when it's on my mind.

I'm not the same as them,
I don't fit in.

But it's all okay,
Because I like being this way.

I am me,
And this is my identity.

Sami Smyth-Omar (10)
Markeaton Primary School, Derby

Weird Animals

F lying pigs eating bacon
A nd if cows can jump over the moon, why can't pigs fly?
N arwhal on a walk, eating crabs
T riceratops eating watermelon
A lligators dancing with crocodiles
S loth is supersonic
Y ou exercising your dog.

Seth Clark
Markeaton Primary School, Derby

Thoughts

Am I one of a kind?
Am I one of the stars up above?
Do I fit in?
Shall I listen to haters?
Shall I stay happy or listen to the comments?
All these thoughts are running through my head.
Is it all true?

Everyone has a point in life!
But do I...?

Alice Miles (9)
Markeaton Primary School, Derby

Princess' Castle

The princess' castle
Is very unknown.
It used to be known,
Until it turned into stone.
The rumours spread and slid,
Like leaves in the wind.
It's covered in vines that lace and swing,
And jagged plants that spike and spin.

Aliyana Macfarlane (9)
Markeaton Primary School, Derby

Fearless

What makes me, me?
I am fearless and kind.
I am not scared to take a risk.
Don't be disrespectful to people and hurt people.
They know that I like friends.
This world is so fearless today.
Is it true to learn about fearlessness?

Lucie Webb (10)
Markeaton Primary School, Derby

Be Proud

A voice stands
Tall like the
Sun,
And beams
Bright in the
Sky,
But is mostly
Overlooked.
I don't care,
My DNA is
Different,
That's what
Makes me
Proud!
Like mountains
In the sky.

Elliott Kinnear (10)
Markeaton Primary School, Derby

Shadows

A voice rises, sure as the sun returning.
Like a mountain that doesn't ask permission to be tall,
Like a flame that doesn't flicker in the wind.
Pride wears no crown but stands tall.
Every shadow knows their shape.

Ariana Evans (10)
Markeaton Primary School, Derby

Cyclops

C lumsy and clever
Y outhful and yearning
C hirpy and sturdy
L egendary and lonely giant
O ne-eyed monster
P etrifying and scary
S tupid and flexible beast.

Arthur Stone (9)
Markeaton Primary School, Derby

My Daily Life

In the morning, I start the day,
Then I go to school.
Unfortunately, it's not that cool.
After school, I go home.
Seriously, leave me alone.
Straight to my house,
I hear my dad clicking a mouse.

William Johnstone (10)
Markeaton Primary School, Derby

Being Me

After school
Swimming on Tuesday
Going home at 4:30
Having a snack
Having tea
Doing my homework
Playing games for a bit
Watching my phone
And repeating this again... and again

Rudra Ashwin (10)
Markeaton Primary School, Derby

Animal!

A roar, a meow and a grunt
N ew cats and calves
I n love with all of nature
M ust act now
A world we need, disappearing
L ives must be saved.

Arthur Toogood (10)
Markeaton Primary School, Derby

My Voice

Everyone
Everybody
They all have one voice
In passion
In love
In a tone
In a song
They all have one voice to have
Everyone except me.

Toby Lince (10)
Markeaton Primary School, Derby

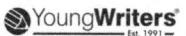

Unique Peace

I'm not a stranger to the dark,
I am like a tiny spark,
I can start a fire,
I'm like a fisherman
Trying to catch
A
Shark!

Jack Rose (10)
Markeaton Primary School, Derby

Amy The Alien!

Amy the alien,
Once South Australian,
Tried to fly to the moon.
The moon was her home,
Where she met her clone,
They even liked the same tune.

Jack Rothwell (10)
Markeaton Primary School, Derby

Outdoor World

Sun shining.
Grass swaying.
Trees swooping.
Children singing.
Bees buzzing.
Phones ringing.
Apples falling.
People sitting.
Balloons flying.
Tables standing.
Bins scraping.

Lexi Deacon (7)
Mayflower Community Academy, Plymouth

All About Nature

N ature all around

A pples crunching

T ulips growing freely everywhere

U ndulating branches blowing in the wind

R ivers gushing

E arwigs scuttling.

Thea Shurmer (7)
Mayflower Community Academy, Plymouth

Summer

S un shining on the beach
U mbrella giving shade
M aking memories
M aking sandcastles
E veryone enjoying themself
R eady to go home.

Mariana Jannetta (7)
Mayflower Community Academy, Plymouth

Heroes

S uper
U nstoppable
P erfect
E xtraordinary
R ole master
H elps
E xcellent
R espectful
O bedient.

Daniella Babatunde (7)
Mayflower Community Academy, Plymouth

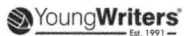

About Animals

Squirrels climbing.
Foxes hunting.
Birds chirping.
Spiders webbing.

Abi Edworthy (7)
Mayflower Community Academy, Plymouth

What Am I?

I fly high in the lazy sky,
The sky flooded with blue.
My wings grow tired with a heavy sigh,
My migration not yet ready, even though I'm working
on it too!

The sun loses height,
As we begin to rest,
The slowly fading light,
While the younger ones have a heaving chest!

The flock has hope,
So have I.
I'm like the Pope.
Though the flock and I are kind of dry!

What am I?

Harmony Chen (8)
Queen's Gate Junior School, London

My Favourite Day ~ Sunday

Sunday is my favourite day
Sunday is the day I play
With all my coins
I get to buy more toys
I get to see my friends
And write with my new pens
I go to bed
Whilst my mum is making bread
And I think in my head
Tomorrow I have school
So no more pools
Because tomorrow is Monday
But right now is still Sunday.

Lily Hurst (7)
Queen's Gate Junior School, London

What Is It?

It's as tall as my French book
It's as yummy as ice cream
It's as chewy as fudge
It's as brown as a box
It's as sweet as honey
It's as peanutty as a monkey nut
It's a Snickers bar!

Evelyn Marini-Goodwin (7)
Queen's Gate Junior School, London

Friends Are Fantastic

Friends are funny,
Filling the day with giggles and games.
We wander, we wonder,
Whispering wild whistles under the willow tree.
Laughter leaps like little leaves,
Spinning in the sunny sky.
Kind hearts know how to care,
Keeping secrets, sharing snacks,
Standing side by side.
When the world feels wobbly,
A friend's face is a shining star.
Friendship is fulfilling,
A forever kind of thing,
Floating like feathers,
In the wide, welcome wind.

Alexandra Stranis (8)
Saffron Green Primary School, Borehamwood

Being Free

F is for a free and fantastic world we live in,
R is for radiant and relaxing schools we go to,
E is for the exciting and excellent pets we have,
E is for the enthusiastic and elegant teachers we
students have,
D is for our delightful and devoted parents we have,
O is for optimistic and open-minded children,
M is for the magical and mythical nature we have.

Sophia Maria Botosanu (9)
Saffron Green Primary School, Borehamwood

ung**Writers**

A Simple Wish

I really wish I had a puppy, a little friend
So I asked my mummy
Oh please, oh please, make my dream come true
He will take care of me, and also you
A big, solid 'No' was her reply
So I sat in the corner and began to cry
Maybe one day I will get a puppy
I'll just have to keep on asking my mummy.

Alaya Neophytou (9)
Saffron Green Primary School, Borehamwood

120

A Penny's Story

A humble disc, a copper gleam,
A penny's story, a simple dream.
Forgotten often, on the ground,
A little treasure to be found.

Tossed in fountains for luck's embrace,
Or saved in jars, a secret place.
A small beginning for fortunes grand,
A tiny coin in a hopeful hand.

Though value small, its meaning vast,
A reminder of moments meant to last.
Of simple joys and childhood glee,
The humble penny for all to see.

So the next time you find one, shining bright,
Remember its journey in the light.
A little piece of history's hold,
The story of a penny, silently told.

Poppy du Parcq (11)
Sheen Mount Primary School, Sheen

Nature

Trees stretched up to the sky,
Mountains were glistening up high,
Cliffs had boulders passing by,
And clouds lay on the sky.

But in all of this wonderful nature,
There was danger,
Starvation,
Deforestation,
Creation vanishing,
And perishing,
But the real danger was in the secrets,
Too shy to unfold,
Too young or old.

Until later, they remained untold,
And soon people found out
Why trees stretched to the sky,
And why mountains glistened up high,
And why cliffs had boulders passing by,
And why clouds lay on the sky,
And now, people started to know
Why.

Cinar Ozcan (11)
Sheen Mount Primary School, Sheen

Rise And Fall

The brightest light
Outshone the darkest night,
All will fall,
No matter how tall.
Divine shall dissolve,
New shall evolve,
Bound by love.
One is simply a dove,
But the eternal die,
Even the sky,
At its own pace,
Death and destruction feeds emptiness and space.
You might shine at day,
Or give things away,
Even jump into hay,
But at the end of time,
None shall do the crime
Of staying in their prime.
None shall fend off their fall,
No matter how much they stall,
But even the strongest, who live the longest,
Have an ending, like this poem.

Eric Net (11)
Sheen Mount Primary School, Sheen

The Four Seasons

Winter
The air is cold,
The sky is grey,
Snow falls down,
The Christmas joy.

Spring
The air warms up,
The sun starts to shine,
Blossom falls down,
The Easter joy.

Summer
The air is warm,
The sun beams down,
The flowers fall,
The beach joy.

Autumn
The air gets cooler,
The clouds cover sun,
The leaves fall down,
The Halloween fun.

Then winter comes round again,
Those are the four seasons,
They repeat like that forever,
Until the very end.

Charlotte Boyd (10)
Sheen Mount Primary School, Sheen

Deerfox

Oh, great deerfox, you are so rare
Always standing bold up there
In the starlit sky, you rise
Giving tiger cubs a surprise

You rule all time and space
Through your portals, you race
To be the first to see
The new world with glee

Your fur is soft and smooth
You walk in long strides, which is how you move
Up in the Aurora Borealis, which is your phone
With the leader of the deerfoxes on the throne

Mystical, magical, that is you
You are the deerfox.

Florence Ferrer (10)
Sheen Mount Primary School, Sheen

Above The Sky...

Up high, where not much was known,
Planets orbit with lots of aura,
But still...
To this day...
No one knew about its order.
Luckily, to this day, someone wondered,
What's above the sky? He looked up...
Mesmerised.

Now, people look up high with a bright gleam in their
eye...
Knowing the deepest, darkest secrets...

Ryan Price (11)
Sheen Mount Primary School, Sheen

The Fire Phoenix

Burning bright
Through the night,
Flying high
In the sky.

Screeching, scorching,
Billowing, burning,
Tossing, turning,
A red-hot warning.

But through the times,
It always shines,
Glowing with warmth and joy.

Alexandra Kaoullas (11)
Sheen Mount Primary School, Sheen

Nature

I can see blosson upon the trees,
And fruit, "Mmm, yes, if you please!"

There are little fish in the pond,
Because animals are really fond of the pond.

I can hear the swaying trees
In the warm breeze.

In the morning, I can hear
Some tweeting in my ear.

I can smell the lovely flowers
Blooming in the flower fields.

I can feel the tickly butterflies flying to and fro,
With their colours glistening in the glowing show!

Ivy Brown (7)
Shipbourne School, Shipbourne

Love

Love
Is a warm and fuzzy feeling,
And helps you think
You can do anything.

Love
Makes everything feel okay,
Even on the most
Difficult days.

Love
Can pick you up
When you're feeling sad,
And leave you feeling
Especially glad.

Love
Is a cuddle and kiss
Any time of the day,
And helps you know
That everything is okay.

Love
Is happy,
Red and bright,
And reassures you
Everything is alright.

Love
Lifts you high
In the sky,
Without you needing
To ask why.

Love
Is not leaving you
In any muddle,
And with a glow in your heart,
And lots of cuddles.

Eleanor Walton (8)
Shipbourne School, Shipbourne

The World Of Football

I can see footballs being kicked about,
They're having fun, there is no doubt.

They watch football on TV,
When they score, they're very pleased.

Many colours running around,
I can hear boots charging on the ground.

I can see a man scoring a goal,
The crowd cheers, "Yay!" as a whole.

They say, "Good game," after the match,
And on the pitch, there is a big muddy patch.

Alistair Gibbon (8)
Shipbourne School, Shipbourne

One Night

One day, at night
I saw an amazing sight
I peered through the door
And saw a cat and a macaw
It seemed to be a meeting
As they gave each other greetings
The cat wore a hat
The hat was very fat
And it covered the cat's eyes
The macaw was learning the alphabet, violin
And how to swim
We all met and had a cup of hot chocolate
And looked at flags too.

Zara Lyons (8)
Shipbourne School, Shipbourne

Friends For Life

Friends for life
Friends are kind
In the light for life
But if you fight
You will get very tired.

Friends for life
They make me smile
They play games
And make me laugh.

Friends for life
Let's all have fun!

Jasmine Fox (8)
Shipbourne School, Shipbourne

Jellyfish

Jellyfish wiggle like jelly,
Jellyfish wash up on the sandy beach,
Jellyfish are unbelievably slimy,
Jellyfish sting like stinging nettles,
Moonlight glowing jellyfish,
Jellyfish are like colourful candyfloss!

James Ruse (8)
Shipbourne School, Shipbourne

Summer

S uper fun park trips,
U nlimited ice creams,
M usic playing at the seaside,
M any children in the pool,
E veryone being happy,
R unning on the beach.

Joey Levett (8)
Shipbourne School, Shipbourne

The Super Happy Snow

The snow made a cloudy mist,
It kisses so hard, and never misses,

It sprinkles down just like flour,
And covers every steeple and tower.

The snow is like a blanket floating to the ground,
And children make snowmen as it swirls around.

Snowflakes fall upon your face with the bitterly cold of winter.
The snow likes cold hugs, and never likes warm snugs.

The snow always turns up for the Christmas fun,
And it never wants to leave until it's done.

The snow enjoys Christmas carols,
It rolls around like knocked-down barrels.

The snow is so happy and full of delight,
When it eventually melts, it's full of fright.

Can't wait to see you again, Happy Snow!

Poppy Strike (9)
St Joseph's Catholic Primary School, Thame

The Storm!

The lightning was a one-second dance,
Everyone started to prance.
People thought it was very frightening,
It was like a beam of light brightening.

The storm was a monster coming into your room,
It was starting to become doom.
The thunder started to laugh,
Its power cut the sky in half.

The light was a ray, waking the city,
People were saying, "That's pretty!"
It was like a shining ring,
The light was the king.

People were screaming, their town was on fire,
The scene was like a funeral pyre.
All because of the flash,
Buildings were starting to crash.

Toby Partner (9)
St Joseph's Catholic Primary School, Thame

When Floods Come

When floods come,
Ducks feel delighted, people run.
Water is free for it fought, dry space is none.

When floods come,
The clouds are stretched,
The flood, speeding conveyor belts.
On faces, worry is etched.
Suddenly, merriment melts.

When floods come,
Liquid charges at the city like an army,
Every drop, soldiers at war.
The tension is enough to make anyone barmy.
People freeze still, as if it were law.

When floods come,
Homes are destroyed.
Water is ruthless.
Emergency minds are deployed.
The city is left speechless.

Florrie Hollis (9)
St Joseph's Catholic Primary School, Thame

How The Sun Saved The Flower

The flower longed for a good time,
The flower longed for the sunshine,
The petals were as cold as ice,
Winter just didn't feel nice.
Through the darkness and through the night,
The flower was a knight
Trying to fight,
Then the sun came,
And didn't have shame.

The sun shone bright,
The flower didn't have fright
Because the sun has shone,
Now it's the most kind.
The shining sun made the flower grow,
Now tall,
Not low,
Now big and strong,
And long.
The flower is as big as a tower.
The sun has the power!

Theia Perry (9)
St Joseph's Catholic Primary School, Thame

Hurricane: The Dreaded

The hurricane,
The dreaded pain,
The old-fashioned cane,
The prison chain,
The hurricane.

It's a runner sprinting without heavy breath,
Clamping us together in a big huddle,
Casting us to our only death,
In a dangerously tight cuddle.

It's a hairdryer blowing our hair,
Even if we cling,
All it does is tear and tear,
And rip up everything.

Wait, what's that?
A strong ray of sun!
Of course, we completely forgot,
That sunshine is the predator,
Hurricane is the prey.

Maeve Talbot (9)
St Joseph's Catholic Primary School, Thame

Northern Lights In The Sky!

Northern Lights are very bright,
They always come in first light,
The light was like a divine being,
People thought it was very exciting.
Phones' light like a star in the dark sky.

It looked like a person
Painted a painting on a black canvas.
The Northern Lights were like a goddess,
Entering the universe called Aurora Borealis.
The colours were a rainbow in the night.
People said it was enchanting to see.
Photos faked, children amazed,
Now they may say, "I'll never forget."

Gabriela Glazer (9)
St Joseph's Catholic Primary School, Thame

Weather

Oh look, here's a cloud,
Soft, cotton candy in the sky,
People hope they're allowed
To eat it all, I'll cry.

Oh look, here's the sun,
Shining peacefully on us,
The sun can be fun,
Let's hope for no fuss.

Oh look, here's a rainbow
Shining brightly through,
Who was beginning to be aglow,
It was a dream come true.

Oh look, here's the lightning,
A flash of light in the sky,
For some, it's frightening,
Making them cry.

Ashlee Sinclair (9)
St Joseph's Catholic Primary School, Thame

When The Rainbow Glows

When the rainbow glows,
Rain has gone away,
Sun has come,
Everyone is happy again.

When the rainbow glows,
The colours high and bright
Across the sapphire sky,
Making everyone scream with pride.

When the rainbow glows,
The colour appears
To show the storm disappeared,
There's nothing to fear.

When the rainbow glows,
Treasure is near,
Making everyone filled with colourful cheer,
The rain gets jealous and pokes it with a spear.

Katy Wright (9)
St Joseph's Catholic Primary School, Thame

When The Lightning Strikes

When the lightning strikes,
The brightness fades away.

When the lightning strikes,
People run, animals hiding.

When the lightning strikes,
The clouds envy.

When the lightning strikes,
It is a one-second kick.

When the lightning strikes,
It lingers along.

When the lightning strikes,
It is like a striker kicking the ball.

When the lightning strikes,
It is a frightening sight.

Jasper Darby (9)
St Joseph's Catholic Primary School, Thame

Thunder And Lightning Are Frightening

When the thunder rumbled,
The lightning struck like skating across the sky,
With a bird with wings.

When the lightning strikes,
The thunder was dancing,
One-second dance and being crazy.

When the thunder growled,
The lightning came to play,
And strikes the ground,
And makes the earth waken.

When the lightning strikes,
It pinched the ground,
With all of its might,
And power.

Stanley Quin (8)
St Joseph's Catholic Primary School, Thame

The Frightening Storm

The clouds signalled a storm,
As loud as a blowhorn!
The devil came down and he was a big, black cloud!

The storm was a giant, riling, electric machine gun,
Shooting lightning bolts at the city.
The storm's tummy rumbled.

The city's umbrellas were crying to death
When the sky turned black.
When the clouds saw the storm, they ran before it did
its mighty roar.

Milan Iojica (9)
St Joseph's Catholic Primary School, Thame

Snowland

The snow was a blanket,
The snowflakes were whistling like a racket,
The sand was dead,
The rocks were in bed.

Some squirrels were arguing,
Others having big fun things,
The bugs were on holiday,
Until they drifted away.

Death in o' the wintertime,
Wasn't like o' the great summertime,
Like the dark nighttime,
Which was a fine fright-time.

Benji Jurik (9)
St Joseph's Catholic Primary School, Thame

Thunder And Lightning

When it thunders, the lightning strikes the ground
Like a massive boat hitting the ground
And making everything shake.

The clouds form, people go inside
And people get sad
Even though it's entertaining, we all get scared!

The lightning is a one-second rock song
Scaring everyone to bits
Everyone goes into the kitchen
So the lightning entertains us.

James Constant (8)
St Joseph's Catholic Primary School, Thame

The Hailstorm

Pieces of hail are small,
The hail was very hard,
As small as a snail,
As hard as a nail (very hard).

All the hail pieces formed as a prism,
Hail hit me and I was very sad,
It was very hard to bail,
And then I wailed a lot.

The hail is in a straight line,
The hail is sliding rapidly,
Because it is in a trail,
Because it is on a big rail.

Jack Andre Arthur Markham (9)
St Joseph's Catholic Primary School, Thame

When The Trees Dance

When the trees dance,
The people prance,

When the trees dance,
The monkeys go to France.

When the trees dance,
The frogs have romance,

When the trees dance,
The sun creates a trance.

When the trees dance,
It is like a waterfall of green,

When the trees dance,
They like to be seen.

Max Weller (9)
St Joseph's Catholic Primary School, Thame

The Sun Shines

When the sun shines,
People eat delicious things.

When the sun shines,
The sun gives me a warm hug.

When the sun shines,
Rabbits love to come out.

When the sun shines,
The sun is a hot water bottle.

When the sun shines,
Children have fun.

When the sun shines,
Clouds run away.

Juliet Peddle (9)
St Joseph's Catholic Primary School, Thame

The Hail And Snow Are Falling

The hail is falling,
The snail is cooling.

The hail is falling,
The mail is boring.

The hail is falling,
The whale is roaring.

The hail is falling,
The detail is crawling.

The snow is falling,
It blows in the morning.

The snow is falling,
The yeti is a warning.

Thomas Carpenter (9)
St Joseph's Catholic Primary School, Thame

The Snow Melting Away

When the snow falls,
Everything turns to white.
Be careful, don't get frostbite.

When the snow falls,
It clearly gains height.
The people rise,
Right in our eyes.

When the snow falls,
It travels through the air,
It melts away, like it's attacked a bear.

Alex Karpovych (9)
St Joseph's Catholic Primary School, Thame

When The Snow Falls

When the snow falls,
Sun stops, goosebumps grow.

When the snow falls,
Snowflakes drop, winds blow.

When the snow falls,
Majestic icicles glow.

When the snow falls,
Spirits raise, reindeer neigh.

When the snow falls,
Christmas rules!

Matilda Stubbs (9)
St Joseph's Catholic Primary School, Thame

Four Seasons

Spring is here,
It's time to cheer,
Cherry trees blossom,
It's almost like winter is forgotten.
Daffodils rise high like the sun,
Time for the children to have some fun.
In farmers' fields where the sky is blue,
Lambs frolic around like a happy crew.

Summer, summer, so lovely and hot,
We might get some rain, but let's hope not.
Longer days are here, and there's no more school.
Instead, we eat ice lollies and try to stay cool.
Swimming in a pool until the sun goes down,
Beaches and barbecues, and late-night strolls around
town.

Autumn time, it's time for a change,
When the clocks go back, it's really strange.
Leaves fall off the trees and make a mess,
Yellow, orange and red, these colours are the best.
Cooler and darker nights are drawing in,
It's time for the harvest to begin.

Winter has come, so expect some snow,
It feels like summer was a long time ago.
Animals hibernating and icy lakes,
The crunchy snow, I like the sound it makes.
The days are short and the nights are long,
Scarves, gloves and coats, everyone has them on.
Frozen fingers, frozen toes,
Time for winter to come to a close.

Maddison Crook (9)
St Nicholas CE (VA) Primary School And Nursery, Stevenage

The Months

January brings the snow,
Makes feet and fingers glow.

February brings the rain,
Freezes the lakes again.

March brings the wind,
And stirs the daffodils.

April makes us twirl around,
Making daisies whoosh around.

May brings flocks of pretty lambs,
Making us jump up and down.

June brings lilies, roses and daffodils,
As pretty as can be.

Hot July brings cool and showers,
Apricots and gillyflowers.

August is the best of all,
When harvest is home in all.

Warm September lets us free,
From having a shower spree.

Fresh October brings us more,
Like pumpkins and all that sort.

Dull November gives a blast,
When all the leaves are red.

Cold December gives us cheer,
Santa Claus has been here.

Sara Szilagyi (9)
St Nicholas CE (VA) Primary School And Nursery, Stevenage

The Magical Wonders

A colourful rainbow in the sky
A sparkly gold star
A fluffy soft cloud
The song of a violin
The cutest dog
And the bluest bluebells.

The coldest pretty snowflake of winter
The orangest autumn leaf
The first flower of spring
The hottest weather in summer.

The fluffiest yellow and black bee
A red rose full of beauty
A fluffy grey cat with the longest fur
The yellowest, gold, soft sands
The bluest water from the sea
A planet.

Poppy Lasenby (9)
St Nicholas CE (VA) Primary School And Nursery, Stevenage

Once I Saw A Fairy

I was playing with my friend, and his name was Barky. He jumped up and down with a big smile of joy. He came to me and said, "I think I saw a fairy!" Then we both jumped up and down, smiles filling our faces. I suddenly just said, "Let's go on a fairy hunt!" Barky thought it was dangerous to go! But I... didn't think so! We both went deeper in the woods until we saw a magic door! I peeked through first and I saw a fairy! Then I thought, *Is it just one fairy?*

Ming Yee Tsang (8)
St Nicholas CE (VA) Primary School And Nursery, Stevenage

Would You Be My Friend If...?

Would you be my friend if
I'd never share anything
I'd always talk too much
I'd talk as loud as a drum and as quick as my thumb
could go down
I'd always accidentally trip over you
I'd always play with someone else
I'd always talk over you
I'd never reply to you
Would never help you?

But what if I was the opposite?
Would you be my friend?
Would you be my friend if I was kind and helpful?

Ella Fawibe (9)
St Nicholas CE (VA) Primary School And Nursery, Stevenage

Friends Forever!

In the garden of life,
Friends bloom like flowers bright,
Their laughter and warmth,
A comforting light.
Through joys and sorrows,
They stand by our side,
In their embrace,
Our fears and doubts subside.
They're the stars that twinkle in our darkest night,
Guiding us forward with their love so bright.
With them, every moment turns into a treasure,
And that's what friends are...
Forever!

Pyper De Jager (9)
St Nicholas CE (VA) Primary School And Nursery, Stevenage

Friendship

F orever having each other's backs
R elying on each other
I nspiring each other, step by step
E verlasting memories
N ever forgotten moments
D reams shared and achieved
S upportive when times are rough
H elping others when things are tricky
I nseparable and always together
P rotecting others when things are scary.

Estera Vasiliu (8)
St Nicholas CE (VA) Primary School And Nursery, Stevenage

My Friendship

What am I?
We are the people who play
Having fun lasts every day
We share a bond so strong
Together, we can't go wrong
We come as two or many
To anyone, it costs a penny
Days filled with so much laughter
But we always make sure we are looked after.

Brodie Coveney (8)
St Nicholas CE (VA) Primary School And Nursery, Stevenage

Monkey Life

I am a monkey swinging through the trees,
Look up high, and that's where I will be.
I wish the times would never end,
And tomorrow will be the time to play again.
I am going to sleep, and in the morning,
I will do the same thing again and again.

Milo Cleverdon (9)

St Nicholas CE (VA) Primary School And Nursery, Stevenage

The Monkey Tree

A monkey on its tail,
Hanging up high,
With breeze and wind blowing through the leaves,
And gold...

Angel Ayomide Ojo (9)
St Nicholas CE (VA) Primary School And Nursery, Stevenage

Growing Up

G rateful, born I was on a great starry night,

R ealise how fast you'd be tucking me in tight,

O bject, how quickly I'd start to grow up,

W onder if I'd grow to give up,

I nspiration, you gave me courage to grow up with a warm heart,

N aturally, I had to go get a job and be able to depart,

G ain confidence and gather enough money to get a stunning house.

U nique, my growing journey carrying on as I hold my little pet mouse,

P onder, up in the sky as I fly high.

Hollie Jenkins (11)
Ulceby St Nicholas Church Of England Primary School, Ulceby

Friendship

F riends, you see their laughs and smiles

R ealise their scent from a mile

I feel their hand as we skip around in circles

E pic is the word to describe our favourite animal, turtles

N ice is what all friends are, no matter what

D on't worry, your friends will always be there, even if you get a cut

S un is like a friend, friends follow you wherever you go

H onesty always glows

I ncredible what friends truly are

P erfect like friendship because friends are stars.

Maisie Webb (11)

Ulceby St Nicholas Church Of England Primary School, Ulceby

I'm A Banana

As a banana, you grow on a tree,
My bunch was the place for me.
Coconuts, so hard and high,
They watch all the bananas slowly die.

Cocoa pods and nuts make chocolate nuts,
They are taken inside small huts.
There are fields behind the huts with wheat and rye,
They're being harvested by a great, big combine.

At the supermarket where bananas are sold,
The freezer aisle is way too cold.
The fruit aisle is the place for me,
This is the place I'll always be.

Edward Paul (11)
Ulceby St Nicholas Church Of England Primary School, Ulceby

Solar System

S o, eight planets, let's get it right
O rbiting the sun, having lots of fun
L uminous stars in the sky
A stronauts looking for alien life
R ushing to find us ET life

S piralling galaxy in the sky
Y et we can't see them from Earth
S ince they're so, so far away
T he solar system is full of planets
E gg shapes and spheres
M ars is my favourite planet as it shows no fear.

Oscar Montgomery (11)
Ulceby St Nicholas Church Of England Primary School, Ulceby

One Amazing Friend

One amazing friend can make you smile,
Even when it's been a long, long while;
Sometimes, when I'm feeling sad,
I think of the tremendous adventures we've had.

Even with all the odds and ends,
We will always be the best of friends,
Now your friend is near,
They will always be here, never fear.

They will always mean everything,
More than the dark side of the ring.

Tilly Butler (10)
Ulceby St Nicholas Church Of England Primary School, Ulceby

Truckfest

T he only place on Earth I want to be.

R oaring of the engines rumbles around the showground.

U nder the beaming sun,

C ool glasses flash.

K nowing there are shows to come,

F eel the excitement!

E very engine is a work of art.

S ounds of the crowd screaming and cheering,

T he event is here; it's Truckfest!

Trystan Reed (11)
Ulceby St Nicholas Church Of England Primary School, Ulceby

Baby Crow

B aby crows hatching all around
A lthough this little crow is different
B aby crow limping and struggling with a broken wing
Y oung one, stop trying to fly, you're falling within seconds.

C rows circling me
R ound and round
O ver my head
W here I was, the crow was hiding, deep in my shadow.

Oakley Whall (11)
Ulceby St Nicholas Church Of England Primary School, Ulceby

Football

As I play football and I dream,
And after that, I get an ice cream,
But through the summer, I can play,
I can play, just play all day,
Because I'm tall and a good striker,
I could also be a good biker,
While I play in my garden,
I keep burping, so I say pardon,
The more I score, the more I shout,
And I will play forever, no doubt.

Ollie Cade (10)
Ulceby St Nicholas Church Of England Primary School, Ulceby

Sunflowers

The sun comes out of its small winter's cave,
My skin now becomes its slave.
Green shoots pop up from the ground,
The sun becomes their main background.
The shoots grow taller, yellow petals appear,
The tips of the leaves point like a spear.
We're nearly there, I dance and cheer,
My sunflower garden, fully grown for the year.

Jessica Ransom (10)
Ulceby St Nicholas Church Of England Primary School, Ulceby

Tralalero Tralala

The shark, deep under the waters,
Wagging its tail, searching for a fish,
Spots one while licking his lips,
Patiently waiting for a dish of fish and chips.

The shark is now about to dig in,
Excited, as you could tell from his large fin,
Couldn't finish it, so it went in the bin.

Oscar Greer (10)
Ulceby St Nicholas Church Of England Primary School, Ulceby

Fluffy Dandelion

Fluffy dandelion flew away,
Ready for another day,
When its seeds begin to sprout,
A sea of yellow flowers comes out.

Graceful dandelion drifts through the breeze,
Tickling my nose and making me sneeze,
I hope you venture far and wide,
But always be in my mind.

Willow Zergi (10)
Ulceby St Nicholas Church Of England Primary School, Ulceby

The Unknown

Within me, there is dust,
Flying rocks bust.
There is a lot of fear,
But I'm not clear.
Lots of people wonder,
I'm surrounded by thunder.
I have a lot of space,
But I don't have a base.

What am I?
I may be space/a galaxy.

Ellie-Rose Whitham (11)
Ulceby St Nicholas Church Of England Primary School, Ulceby

Lonely Cloud Gets A Friend

One day, there was a cloud,
And she wasn't very loud.
The cloud didn't have a friend,
So she didn't blend.
Another cloud came along,
And they belong.
They never left each other's side,
And didn't hide.
Together,
Forever.

Jorgie Lewis (10)
Ulceby St Nicholas Church Of England Primary School, Ulceby

Micoli

M essy and never cleans up his room.
I gnorant and lazy.
C harming and joyful.
O ccasionally stays in his room.
L emonade is one of his favourite drinks.
I dentical to me and the same eye colour.

Sebastian Drozdowicz (10)
Ulceby St Nicholas Church Of England Primary School, Ulceby

My BFF

D ancing freely through the night
E very day, we freely dance
N urturing friendships
N aming the foods of the world
I n every heartbeat, a story told
S miles wherever anyone goes.

Josh Easton (9)

Ulceby St Nicholas Church Of England Primary School, Ulceby

Boden

B eats me and my brothers up
O nly he is allowed to watch anything related to Batman
D oes not like company from his brothers
E ntertains us when he's enraged
N ever lets go of Wotsits.

Roman Cowie (10)
Ulceby St Nicholas Church Of England Primary School, Ulceby

The Universe

S tars glowing bright in the dead of night
P eople in space, rockets take flight
A s I fly, the darkness never leaves me alone
C ould I live in the unknown?
E very second, I think of home.

Henry Greer (9)
Ulceby St Nicholas Church Of England Primary School, Ulceby

Roblox

R eady to play,
O n goes my orange, new headset,
B oys, we are going to win!
L et's go into the fight,
O ver and over again,
X box got the least kills, we win!

Theo Butler (10)
Ulceby St Nicholas Church Of England Primary School, Ulceby

Fortnite

F ortnite is
O utstanding, built
R eally for
T he best,
N ow that
I t's a real
T est, that's tremendously
E xciting, made for all.

Bailey Hinchliffe (9)
Ulceby St Nicholas Church Of England Primary School, Ulceby

Roblox

R eally funny

O ver a hurdle of time

B lockhead

L et's go

O n with the headphones

X for game over.

Mason Stearman (9)
Ulceby St Nicholas Church Of England Primary School, Ulceby

All About My Cat

My cat looks like a sunny day,
My cat sounds like a loud meow,
My cat smells like a tin of cat food,
My cat tastes like a ball of cat hair.

Sophie Spicer (9)
Ulceby St Nicholas Church Of England Primary School, Ulceby

My Superpowers

Some things about me
Are that I have autism and ADHD
I'll tell you what that really means

Some people think it means I'm too loud
But that's not what it's all about
People say I'm too naughty
But their accusations are faulty

It means I think outside the box
And I fidget quite a lot
It doesn't mean I'm not proud of who I am
It just means others need to understand.

Jessica Lee (9)
Woodham Ley Primary School, Great Tarpots

YOUNG WRITERS INFORMATION

We hope you have enjoyed reading this book – and that you will continue to in the coming years.

If you're the parent or family member of an enthusiastic poet or story writer, do visit our website **www.youngwriters.co.uk/subscribe** and sign up to receive news, competitions, writing challenges and tips, activities and much, much more! There's lots to keep budding writers motivated!

If you would like to order further copies of this book, or any of our other titles, then please give us a call or order via your online account.

Young Writers
Remus House
Coltsfoot Drive
Peterborough
PE2 9BF
(01733) 890066
info@youngwriters.co.uk

Join in the conversation!
Tips, news, giveaways and much more!

f YoungWritersUK   **X** YoungWritersCW
◎ youngwriterscw   **♪** youngwriterscw

**Scan to watch
the video!**